O9-AIG-740

Global Issues

Overpopulation

Cheryl Jakab

Smart Apple Media

Smart Apple Media
2140 Howard Drive West
North Mankato, Minnesota 56003

First published in 2007 by
MACMILLAN EDUCATION AUSTRALIA PTY LTD
627 Chapel Street, South Yarra, Australia 3141

Visit our Web site at www.macmillan.com.au or go directly to www.macmillanlibrary.com.au

Associated companies and representatives throughout the world.

Library of Congress Cataloging-in-Publication Data

Jakab, Cheryl.
    Overpopulation / by Cheryl Jakab.
    p. cm. — (Global issues)
    Includes index.
    ISBN 978-1-59920-127-6
    1. Overpopulation—Juvenile literature. 2. Overpopulation—Economic aspects—Juvenile literature.   I. Title.

    HB883.J34 2007
    363.9'1—dc22

                                                            2007004590

Edited by Anna Fern
Text and cover design by Cristina Neri, Canary Graphic Design
Page layout by Domenic Lauricella and Cristina Neri
Photo research by Legend Images
Illustrations by Andrew Louey; graphs by Raul Diche
Maps courtesy of Geo Atlas

Printed in U.S.

Acknowledgements
The author and the publisher are grateful to the following for permission to reproduce copyright material:

Front cover inset photograph: Crowds at the Nakamise, Asakusa, Japan, © James B. Adson/Shutterstock.
Earth photograph courtesy of Photodisc.

Background photograph of Earth and magnifying glass image both courtesy of Photodisc.

AusAid, photo by Peter Ellis, p. 22; AusAid, photo by Jo Elsom, pp. 6 (bottom), 20, 21; BigStockPhoto, p. 11 (bottom); © Freezingpictures/Dreamstime.com, p. 11 (top); © Sivanagk/Dreamstime.com, p. 25; Rebecca Hallas/ Fairfaxphotos, p. 23; Bertrand Guay/AFP/Getty Images, p. 29; AFP PHOTO/Manan Vatsyayana/Getty Images, p. 5; Serge Attal/Time Life Pictures/Getty Images, pp. 6 (left), 13; Robert Nickelsberg/Time Life Pictures/ Getty Images, pp. 7 (bottom), 27; Photodisc, p. 18; Photolibrary, p. 15; © James B. Adson/Shutterstock, p. 12; © Jack Cronkhite/Shutterstock, pp. 6 (top), 16; © Thomas Nord/Shutterstock, p. 14; © OlgaLis/Shutterstock, p. 24; © Vova Pomortzeff/Shutterstock, p. 17; © Michel Stevelmans/Shutterstock, pp. 7 (right), 9; Wikipedia, p. 19.

Please note
At the time of printing, the Internet addresses appearing in this book were correct. Owing to the dynamic nature of the Internet, however, we cannot guarantee that all these addresses will remain correct.

Contents

Glossary words
When a word is printed in **bold**, you can look up its meaning in the glossary on page 31.

Facing global issues

Hi there! This is Earth speaking. Will you take a moment to listen to me? I have some very important things to discuss.

We must face up to some urgent environmental problems! All living things depend on my environment, but the way you humans are living at the moment, I will not be able to keep looking after you.

The issues I am worried about are:
- the huge number of people on Earth
- the supply of clean air and water
- wasting resources
- energy supplies for the future
- protecting all living things
- **global warming** and **climate change**

My global challenge to you is to find a **sustainable** way of living. Read on to find out what people around the world are doing to try to help.

Fast fact

In 2005, the **United Nations Environment Program** Report, written by experts from 95 countries, concluded that 60 percent of the Earth's resources are being **degraded** or used unsustainably.

What's the issue?
World population

In 1999, the population on Earth grew to over 6 billion. That's six thousand million people. How to provide for all the people living on Earth is one of the biggest global environmental issues today.

Providing for all

The environment on Earth must provide people with everything they need—food, water, and shelter. No one really knows how many people Earth can provide for. Whatever the number, there is a limit beyond which Earth will be overpopulated.

Tracking the increase

It is important to keep track of the human population increase so overpopulation can be avoided. Knowing the actual population is the first step to making sure all people can get what they need to survive and live well.

Fast fact
In 2005, more than 250 people were born every minute, increasing the world population by over 80 million per year.

With over a billion people, India is the second most populous country, after China.

Population issues

Around the globe, population issues include:

- the rapid growth in the number of people (see issue 1)
- providing for people in huge cities (see issue 2)
- building over farmland and natural **habitats** (see issue 3)
- poverty and disease, particularly in **developing countries** (see issue 4)
- ways to control population size (see issue 5)

Arctic Circle

N O R T H

A M E R I C A

Mexico

ISSUE 3

Egypt
Building over valuable farmland in the Nile Valley. See pages 16–19.

S O U T H

A M E R I C A

S O U

A T L A

O C E

ISSUE 2

Mexico
Mexico City is one of the poorest mega-cities. See pages 12–15.

ISSUE 4

Southern Africa
People living in extreme poverty and disease. See pages 20–23.

around the globe

Fast fact
Population issues are particularly urgent in Asia, which is home to more than half the world's population.

ARCTIC OCEAN

Arctic Circle

EUROPE

ASIA

China

Egypt

India

AFRICA

ISSUE 1

China
The country with the largest number of people. See pages 8–11.

Equator

AUSTRALIA

Tropic of Capricorn

ANTARCTICA

ISSUE 5

India
Learning how to control population growth. See pages 24–27.

7

The population explosion

Throughout the 1900s, the world population increased so fast it is now described as a population explosion. Today, it appears there may be too many people alive for the resources available.

One billion to six billion

It took human history until about 1850 for the world population to reach one billion. Then, by 1900, there were over 1.5 billion people living on Earth. By 1950, the population reached 2.5 billion. Since then, the population has more than doubled, reaching 6 billion in 1999. The world population is still rising fast.

Too many people

The population explosion led to the world population being too great for the resources available. This has caused many problems throughout the world, including poverty, starvation, famines, disease, wars, and poor living conditions.

Fast fact
Some of the main causes of the population explosion were improved food production, **hygiene**, and medicine.

The world population has now reached over 6 billion.

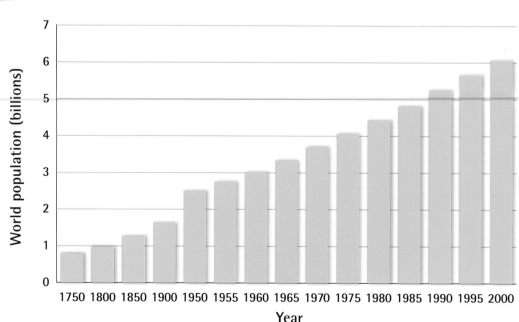

China has more people than any other country.

CASE STUDY
China—the world's largest population

China was the first country in world history to have a population of one billion people. China reached one billion in 1982, just over a hundred years after the population of the whole world had reached a billion.

By 2005, China's estimated population was somewhere around 1.3 billion people. The exact number is unknown, as many births in China go unrecorded. China's population nearly doubled between 1953 and 1982.

China's population growth

Year	Estimated population
1953	582,600,000
1964	694,580,000
1982	1,008,180,000

Asia's population

Five of the ten countries with the largest populations in the world are in Asia. As well as China, many other Asian countries are experiencing rapid population growth.

Top ten largest populations

Rank	Country	Continent
1	China	Asia
2	India	Asia
3	U.S.	North America
4	Indonesia	Southeast Asia
5	Brazil	South America
6	Pakistan	Asia
7	Bangladesh	Asia
8	Russia	Europe
9	Nigeria	Africa
10	Japan	Asia

Toward a sustainable future: Understanding the population explosion

Overpopulation causes environmental damage and poor living conditions. For a sustainable future, people must understand how the population explosion occurred and avoid their numbers growing too fast.

Causes of the population explosion

Since the late 1800s, there have been improvements in food production, hygiene, and medicine. This has enabled more people to survive through childhood and to live long enough to have children of their own. Their children also survived to have their own children, increasing the population at a very rapid rate. Until modern medicine and farming techniques were developed, the population was growing, but at a much slower rate than during the 1900s.

Predicting future population

It is important to know if the population will continue to grow "explosively." At what rate will the population be growing in 10, 20, or 50 years? How much food and other resources will be needed? No one can know for sure what the world population will be in 2020 or 2050, which makes planning for the future very uncertain.

This graph shows one of the lower estimates for future world population.

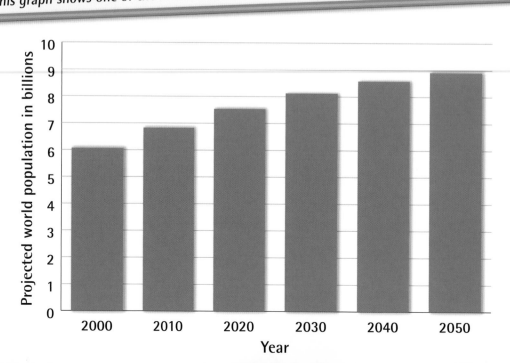

CASE STUDY
Standard of living

Some people have a poor standard of living, while others live in much better conditions.

"Standard of living" is the amount of resources that each person has. In a country with a high standard of living, most people are well supplied with all the resources they need, including health care, education, food, water, and energy supplies.

Influences on standard of living

The population growth rate has a great impact on the standard of living that each person in the population can expect.

When a population grows slowly, the standard of living of each individual tends to be higher. There are more resources available to each person.

When the population grows very rapidly, as it did in the 1900s, many people suffer very poor living conditions or standard of living. With a population growing explosively, supply of resources often cannot keep up with the demands of all these people.

Mega-cities

A mega-city is a city with a population greater than 10 million people. Today the number and size of mega-cities in the world are rapidly growing.

Growth of mega-cities

Cities grow into mega-cities as people move to them to get work. Fewer people are doing farm work, which is now done by machines. More and more work is now available in factories, shops, computing, communications, and other businesses in cities.

Fast fact

In 1900, only 12 cities had 1 million or more people. By 1950, there were 83 cities with over 1 million people.

Problems in mega-cities

Often, services in fast-growing cities do not keep up with the increasing population. In many mega-cities, housing and transportation are poorly set up. Water, power, and other services do not reach many of the people, and often the supply of jobs does not keep up with the arrival of workers.

Top ten largest cities in 2006		
City	Country	Population
Tokyo	Japan	34,200,000
Mexico City	Mexico	22,800,000
Seoul	South Korea	22,300,000
New York	U.S.	21,900,000
São Paulo	Brazil	20,200,000
Mumbai	India	19,850,000
Delhi	India	19,700,000
Shanghai	China	18,150,000
Los Angeles	U.S.	18,000,000
Osaka	Japan	16,800,000

Some mega-cities such as Tokyo have good services.

Mega-cities such as Mexico City often have problems with inner-city slums and shanty towns on their outskirts.

CASE STUDY
Mexico City

In 2005, Mexico City was the second largest mega-city in the world. The population of the Mexico City area is estimated at 18 to 22 million. Mexico City has many problems, including traffic, poverty, and pollution.

Extreme poverty

Houses in many of the poor sections of Mexico City are made of whatever materials can be found, such as scraps of wood and metal. Most of this makeshift housing has no electricity or running water. In Mexico City, an estimated one in five houses is not connected to the sewer system and one in four people has no running water.

Pollution problems

Air pollution is particularly bad in Mexico City. The mountains and volcanoes surrounding the city trap polluted air over the city. Poor air quality causes many health problems.

Fast fact
In 2005, Mexico City was estimated to have 50,000 street children, who have no homes at all.

Toward a sustainable future: Sustainable cities

Cities of the future must be sustainable. That means being able to provide for their people without overusing resources or creating wastes that pollute or damage the environment. It may be that there is a limit to the size of a city that can function well.

City planning

Cities need to be planned to provide for the people living in them. A well-planned, sustainable city has good services and is a safe, pleasant place to live. As more and more people are finding work in cities, it is urgent to plan and build to provide for residents now and into the future.

Services for all

Services each person needs include:

- housing
- food
- clean water
- clean air
- drains and toilets
- garbage collections and **recycling**
- electricity or other power sources
- work to make a living
- transportation to move people around efficiently
- healthcare for all
- schools for all children
- recreation

Japan has an excellent public transportation system, which is important for a sustainable city.

CASE STUDY
Greenbelts

Adelaide, Australia is a good example of a city with extensive greenbelts.

Greenbelts are areas of open land surrounding a town or city. In the greenbelt, further development is strictly controlled. The positioning of greenbelts around cities would stop the growth of unplanned mega-cities.

Advantages of greenbelts

Greenbelts limit the spread of **urban** areas, while providing people in cities with natural areas for recreation and sport. They also help in the fight against pollution in urban areas.

Developing greenbelts

The movement toward developing greenbelts took hold in the 1970s. Where there are greenbelts, the quality of life in cities is improved.

As many mega-cities developed, the idea of having belts around the city caught hold as a good solution to the many environmental problems that can arise from cities growing unchecked. Interested groups stopped or controlled the spread of the city area to make the environment healthier to live in.

Building over farmland

As towns and cities get bigger, they cover more and more land. The suburbs around cities tend to spread in what is known as "urban sprawl." In many cases, this urban sprawl covers valuable farmland.

Decreasing farmland

Good quality land for farming is decreasing quickly due to urban sprawl. With less farmland, our ability to produce food decreases. More than 99 percent of the world's food supply comes from the land. Particularly in rich coastal areas, human housing and cities are stopping large areas of good farming land from producing food.

Increasing need for food

The need for food increases as the population grows. Creating new farmland is the reason for most of the world's land clearing today. When land that had been providing food is taken out of production, more farmland must be found to replace it.

Fast fact
Towns, cities, and urban areas are also covering much of the world's best natural habitats.

Urban sprawl is a major cause of decrease in farming land and natural habitats.

Since ancient times, the rich land in the Nile Valley has been farmed to supply food, as shown in this carving of a man with his cow.

CASE STUDY
The Nile Valley

The Nile Valley has been the center of food production in Egypt for thousands of years. Regular flooding of the Nile enriches the soil on the riverbanks. This rich soil is well known for being the source of food for the ancient Egyptians.

The Nile Valley today

As the population increased in the Nile Valley, houses were built over farmland. This led to a decrease in the amount of land being farmed.

The Nile Valley is still very rich land and could still be as valuable in food production. However, with little control on building over the most fertile land, far less can be used for food production today.

Toward a sustainable future: Limiting urban sprawl

One step to a sustainable future is to limit urban sprawl. People must understand the importance of farmland. Without food, a good standard of living is not possible. If all the good farmland is built over, there is no choice except to import food from other countries.

Fast fact

In 2000, the city of Hanoi, Vietnam, produced 80 percent of its own fresh vegetables, 50 percent of pork, poultry, and freshwater fish, as well as 40 percent of eggs, in urban areas.

Sustaining food supplies

The continued production of enough food depends on farming fertile land to produce food. Sustaining food supplies depends on:

- keeping farmland in production
- farming in ways that do not damage the land
- making the best use of the land available

Urban agriculture

Urban agriculture is growing crops, food animals, fish farms, and forests in or around homes in cities. Urban agriculture makes good use of available land. It is part of the sustainable solution to the problem of making sure all people have food supplies.

Growing food in a city garden adds to food supply and improves the environment.

The garden plots and farm animals are looked after by members of the community.

CASE STUDY
Community gardens

Community gardens are on land made available by local councils for people in the community to garden. Today, thousands of city gardeners have plots in community gardens which allow them to enjoy the experience of gardening and growing their own food. Many cities across the world are now developing public land into community farms and gardens to overcome the lack of space to grow food plants.

Benefit of community gardens

Community garden areas provide many benefits to people. They allow people in cities to grow some of their own food and to come in contact with nature. Community gardeners can work together, make friends, and help each other.

Today, governments in cities and towns promote and support community gardens for their residents because:

- they can be enjoyed by everybody
- they are educational
- they make the city environment more pleasant
- they help people in the community make friends
- all these benefits come at a fairly low cost

Poverty and disease

In 2006, more than half the people of the world lived in poverty. Poverty is where people have very low income or none at all. People live in poverty due to a range of reasons, including war, injustice, unfair sharing of goods, natural disasters, and overpopulation.

Problems of poverty

People living in poverty have many problems, including not getting enough to eat or drink and no way to make their own living. Many of these people also have little or no hope of getting education, healthcare, or medicines.

Disease

Disease is a major problem for people living in poverty. Diseases such as malaria, **AIDS**, and other **infectious diseases** are huge concerns in developing countries, particularly in southern Africa. In 2006 the death rate of children in Africa was nearly 15 times that of the **developed countries** such as the U.S. and Australia.

Fast fact
Poverty is now defined as living on less than $2 a day.

Many people, like these children in South Africa, live in extreme poverty.

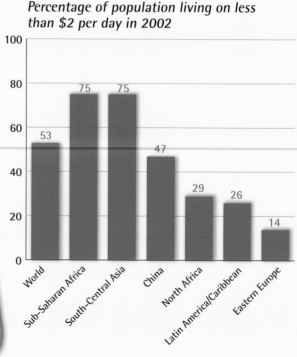

Percentage of population living on less than $2 per day in 2002

Region	Percentage
World	53
Sub-Saharan Africa	75
South-Central Asia	75
China	47
North Africa	29
Latin America/Caribbean	26
Eastern Europe	14

Volunteers go out into the community to educate people about HIV/AIDS.

CASE STUDY
AIDS in Africa

AIDS is a disease that is a major problem in much of the world but particularly in Africa. AIDS is a disease caused by HIV or human immunodeficiency virus. People with HIV who develop AIDS cannot fight off other diseases. Their immune system does not function.

In the following four African countries south of the Sahara Desert, more than 30 percent of the adult population is now infected with HIV:

- Botswana (38.8 percent)
- Lesotho (31 percent)
- Swaziland (33.4 percent)
- Zimbabwe (33.7 percent)

Spread of HIV/AIDS

Today, new HIV infections are decreasing in most developed countries. This drop is mainly due to education about the disease and how it spreads, and medical treatments.

HIV is still spreading rapidly through much of the developing world because of lack of education, health care, and medicines.

Fast fact
More than 30 million people worldwide are infected with AIDS.

Toward a sustainable future: Overcoming poverty

One positive step toward a sustainable future involves providing resources, education, and healthcare to everyone. Many individuals and government and nongovernment agencies worldwide are working towards improving the conditions for those living in poverty.

Identifying rights

Overcoming poverty depends on societies understanding that living in poverty is a denial of basic human rights. In 1948, the United Nations Universal Declaration of Human Rights identified the basic human rights that everyone can expect. One of the most basic rights in that declaration is to be free of poverty. Many people still live their entire lives without these basic rights.

Setting targets

The United Nations Millennium Summit in September 2000 set targets for fighting poverty. By 2015 they are planning to:

- reduce by half the number of people living on less than $1 a day
- provide safe drinking water for 50 percent of people deprived of such access
- reverse the spread of diseases such as malaria and AIDS
- provide primary education for all children

A sustainable future involves controlling poverty and disease for all people, and there is still a long way to go in achieving these targets.

This water supply system will provide safe drinking water to a community in rural East Timor.

Overcoming poverty through fair trade

Many people who live in poverty work hard to make a living but are unable to gain from their hard work. Fair trade occurs when producers get a fair price for their products. Through fair trade, consumers can buy products that were bought at a fair price.

The Fairtrade label

Fairtrade labeling was created in the Netherlands in the late 1980s. The Fairtrade label was launched in 1988 on coffee from Mexico.

The Fairtrade Foundation awards a Fairtrade label to items whose production meets the following standards:

- decent wages, housing, and health and safety are given to workers
- workers have a right to join a union or cooperative
- a fair price is paid to the producer
- the producer supports local social welfare and there is a long-term trading commitment to local producers
- environmentally sustainable production methods are used
- no child labor or forced labor was used to make the product

Fair trade can help overcome poverty rather than being part of the cause of poverty.

The Fairtrade Foundation, with its partners in other countries, checks that products such as coffee continue to meet standards after they have been approved.

The future world population

No one really knows what the world population will be in the future. How many people Earth can support will depend on what new technologies are developed.

More people are now living longer in developing countries.

Living in the 1900s

New farming techniques and advances in medicine that were developed throughout the 1900s led to many changes in living conditions. More food was produced and the standard of living improved for many people.

Living in the 2000s

Across the world, people are now living longer than they did in the past. Average **life expectancy** is increasing, mainly due to improved diet. Many more people are living to very old age. In 2006, more than 300,000 people were over 100 years old and 66 were over 110 years old.

How many people will be living on Earth in 2050? No one knows for certain. Whatever the number, it will have a huge effect on standards of living.

Fast fact
French woman Jeanne-Louise Calment holds the record as the longest lived person ever. She died in 1997, aged 122.

Much of India's population is still rural.

CASE STUDY
India

India is a huge and diverse country with a population of well above a billion people. It is also one of the fastest growing populations. It is rapidly overtaking China as the country with the largest population in the world. India is now developing very fast but many of its people are still among the poorest in the world. India's population growth is having a huge effect on the total world population.

India in 2006

In 2006, India had about 16 percent of the world's population. Many births and deaths are unregistered in India, so numbers can only be estimates.

About one-third of Indians live on or below the poverty line. About three-quarters of the population lives in rural areas with little access to work for money. Average life expectancy is 64 years.

What happens to India's population size in the future will have a huge effect on the total world population.

Toward a sustainable future: Controlling overpopulation

Controlling overpopulation is vital for a sustainable future. The world may already be overpopulated, and the environment might not be able to support the current population properly. A decrease in total population would then be needed for everyone to have a good standard of living.

Developing and developed world

Overall the developed world has a **stable population**, while the developing world population is still increasing. Most of Asia's population is increasing quickly, while overall standards of living and education are low. Europe's population is actually decreasing.

Population control in China

The rate of population growth slowed in China between the 1950s and 1990s due to Chinese government policies. The policies encouraged late marriage and enforced a limit of one child per family. The policy was successful in slowing China's population growth. However, the way the policy was enforced was considered by many people to be against human rights.

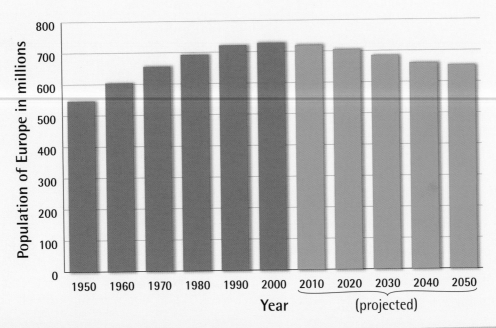

It is projected that Europe's population will decrease.

CASE STUDY
Education for a sustainable population

In 1994, the United Nations identified education as the key to population control and sustainable development. Experience across the world supports the idea that education is the key to population control and a decrease in poverty.

Education of women

Education of women is being used to help control population growth and improve standards of living. Research shows population growth is best controlled by women having access to family planning information.

Family size

Education of women is the best method of limiting family size. When the number of children in a family is smaller, the standard of living of the family improves. This is much better than women having larger numbers of children, many of whom die due to poverty, disease, or famine.

> **Fast fact**
> In 2000, more than one-sixth of the world's population was unable to read or write.

This mobile health and family planning clinic provides birth-control education to rural villagers in India.

What can you do? Sustainable population

You may think that just one person cannot do much, but everyone can help. If every person is careful, the little differences can add up.

Address population issues

Issues of overpopulation, mega-cities, urban sprawl, and poverty are big issues. You may even feel you can do nothing about them. But wherever you live and whatever your situation, you can contribute to a better society. You can make a difference to population issues by:

- donating time or money to help someone less well off than yourself
- using less energy and resources in your daily life
- growing your own or buying locally grown food
- buying products that have been produced and distributed **ethically**
- becoming active in helping protect the rights of others

Join a volunteer organization

After reading about global population issues, you may want to know more about how you can help. Below are a just a few organizations that have been formed by people working for a better and more sustainable future.

Amnesty International

Amnesty International works to protect human rights across the globe. This worldwide pressure group campaigns for the release of all **prisoners of conscience**.

Fast fact
Amnesty International, founded in 1961 by British lawyer Peter Benenson, has about one million members worldwide.

World Wildlife Fund

The World Wildlife Fund is an international voluntary organization devoted to the care and conservation of the natural living world. Its goal is to reverse the degradation of Earth's environment.

United Nations Environment Programme

This United Nations body promotes international cooperation in environmental matters. Its tasks include constant surveillance of the environment in a program called "Earthwatch."

Greenpeace

Greenpeace campaigns to protect the environment. As well as its campaigning work, Greenpeace also funds scientific research and undertakes educational work on environmental issues.

Oxfam Australia

Oxfam is an Australian non-government organization which works in partnership with people in developing countries.

These members of Amnesty International are taking part in a peaceful demonstration in Paris, France, to raise awareness of human rights issues.

Toward a sustainable future

Well, I hope you now see that if you accept my challenge your world will be a better place. There are many ways to work toward a sustainable future. Imagine it . . . a world with:

- a stable climate
- clean air and water
- nonpolluting, **renewable** fuel supplies
- plenty of food
- resources for everyone
- healthy natural environments

This is what you can achieve if you work together with my natural systems.

We must work together to live sustainably. That will mean a better environment and a better life for all living things on Earth, now and in the future.

Web sites

For further information on population and human rights issues, visit these Web sites:

- Amnesty International www.amnesty.org.uk
- Human Rights Watch www.hrw.org
- Population Reference Bureau www.prb.org
- Refugee Action www.refugee-action.org
- Oxfam www.oxfam.org.au/campaigns/mtf/povertyhistory/

Glossary

AIDS
disease of the immune system caused by the human immunodeficiency virus (HIV)

climate change
changes to the usual weather patterns in an area

degraded
run down or reduced to a lower quality

developed countries
countries with industrial development, a strong economy, and a high standard of living

developing countries
countries with less developed industry, a poor economy, and a lower standard of living

ethically
done with principles or standards, within a set of morals

global warming
an increase in the average temperature on Earth

habitats
areas used by living things to provide their needs

hygiene
cleanliness and public health

infectious diseases
diseases that can be spread from one person to another

life expectancy
the length of time a person can expect to live

prisoners of conscience
people held or imprisoned because of their beliefs

recycling
reprocessing a material so that it can be used again

renewable
a resource that can be constantly supplied and which does not run out

rural
areas of low population in the countryside

shanty towns
unofficial settlements

slums
areas with poor living conditions

stable population
a population that stays the same size, neither increasing nor decreasing

sustainable
a way of living that does not use up natural resources

United Nations Environment Program
a program, which is part of the United Nations, set up to encourage nations to care for the environment

urban
area of high population such as towns and cities

Index